Symbols of Plenty

Ruth Bidgood was born in 1922, the daughter of a priest in the Church in Wales. She read English at Oxford and worked as a coder in Alexandria during World War II. She later worked in publishing and began to write poetry following her return to Wales in the 1960s.

One of Wales's leading contemporary poets, this is her tenth published collection of verse.

Also by Ruth Bidgood

Poetry

The Given Time (Christopher Davies, 1972)

Not Without Homage (Christopher Davies, 1975)

The Print of Miracle (Gomer Press, 1978)

Lighting Candles (Seren, formerly Poetry Wales Press, 1982)

Kindred (Poetry Wales Press, 1986)

Selected Poems (Seren, 1992)

The Fluent Moment (Seren, 1996)

Singing to Wolves (Seren, 2000)

New and Selected Poems (Seren, 2004)

Prose

Parishes of the Buzzard (Gold Leaf Publishing, 2000)

Symbols of Plenty

SELECTED LONGER POEMS

Ruth Bidgood

CANTERBURY
PRESS
Norwich

© Ruth Bidgood 2006

First published in 2006 by the Canterbury Press Norwich
(a publishing imprint of Hymns Ancient & Modern Limited,
a registered charity)
9–17 St Alban's Place, London N1 0NX

www.scm-canterburypress.co.uk

The Hymn to Sant Ffraid was commissioned by BBC Wales in
conjunction with the Welsh Arts Council and is reproduced
with permission.

British Library Cataloguing in Publication data

A catalogue record for this book is available
from the British Library

ISBN 1-85311-752 8/978-1-85311-752 7

Typeset by Regent Typesetting, London
Printed and bound by
Bookmarque, Croydon, Surrey

Contents

Acknowledgements

Thanks to the BBC for permission to publish the radio poem *Hymn to Sant Ffraid*, commissioned by BBC Radio Wales in conjunction with the Welsh Arts Council, and broadcast on 5 April 1979.

The sequence 'Land' appeared in *The Fluent Moment* (Seren, 1996), and 'Singing to Wolves' as the title-sequence of a collection (Seren, 2000).

The sequence 'Cwm Pennant', first published by the magazine *Scintilla*, appeared in the anthology *The Hare that Hides Within* (Parthian, 2004).

Earlier versions of 'Riding the Flood' and 'Encounters with Angels' were published by *Scintilla*.

Some individual poems were first published by the following magazines: *David Jones Journal*, *Envoi*, *Interpreter's House*, *New Welsh Review*, *Poetry Wales*, *Scintilla*, *Window on Wales*.

Hymn to Sant Ffraid

This is an ode to a concocted Celtic Saint – concocted in that a real person of whom little is known took on some of the attributes of a previous fertility goddess cum muse, and became the centre of a cult which expressed a number of perennial human preoccupations.

PART I

1st voice   February,
month of Sant Ffraid.
Earth has long lain white, rigid,
locked into lifelessness.
Ice on river, no lively running:
ice on field, no soft furrow:
ice on byre, no boon for beasts:
ice on hill, no high pasture:
ice on heart, no hope leaping.

2nd voice   We call her now to walk on the riverbank,
Brigid of Ireland, Ffraid of Wales, the saint, the
    golden one
who breaks the ice, dipping first one hand, then
    two hands,
freeing the river to flow into time of seed,
time of ripening, time of harvest.
We greet her now, as for so many centuries
winter-starved people greeted her,
from her churches and her wells,
from the cold sea-coast and the doorstep of hill
    farms,
with the immemorial cry—
'Ffraid is come! Ffraid is welcome!'

3rd voice   Ireland was her home, her name there Brigid,
Bride the golden, who would give no man her
    beauty.

3

God was her love, his creatures were her care.
Hers was a magic of giving,
honey for the poor, and cheeses,
yet the shelves were never emptied.
No beggar went from her gate
with unfilled hands or heart.

1st voice   When she left her home, it was not
for any bridegroom of this world,
or for any house but God's.
White-veiled she led her white-robed monks
   and maidens,
blessing Kildare with her living and her dying.
On her tomb fire burned through day and dark,
through years and centuries.

2nd voice   Sant Ffraid, February saint,
unfreezer, unlooser, giver,
saint of the farms, bless now
the year's work starting
with the hard ice melting!

3rd voice   What was she like? It is unfitting to carve her in the cold precision of marble. She was a saint of cloudy western hills, moorland rivers, of sea-brume and secretive islands. Behind that gentle form we dimly see are other shapes that shift in the mist—three or one, three in one: maiden, bride, hag: giver of life, devourer of life: the many-named, the worshipped one, the feared one, Brigid the Goddess, the Mother.

Hymn to Sant Ffraid

1st voice   February,
month of the quickening,
month of Brigid the Threefold,
muse, healer, goddess of fire.
Ice clutches copse and cataract;
earth faints with cold, craves to be free.
In grey of grim dusk,
in black of bleak night,
a cry dies, a life is given.
Blood blots the Bridestone,
flame springs, fire supplicates—
Bride, goddess, bring now
the breaking, the slaking,
the flowing, the growing!

2nd voice   Brigid, the High One,—
She was bringer of corn,
aid-mother of the fecund womb.

3rd voice   Mistress of skills, to her
the merrily-beaten anvil sang
as the forge-fire leapt.

1st voice   Poet and patron of poets, for her
a golden branch all hung with bells
was carried in procession.

2nd voice   She was the leafy bride of May
and the last sheaf of harvest.
To her the girl in travail
on the hut-floor screamed.
The ashes of her fires nourished the fields.

3rd voice   Warriors invoked her healing
with the mouths of their wounds.

2nd voice   She it was exacted
the unchanging price of birth.
'Come to us, White Swan', her children cried,
but feared her, for her gold was red-gold fire,
and within it, darkness.

3rd voice   Winter begged her,
spring thanked her,
summer flaunted her,
autumn gathered her,
and into herself,
into darkness within fire,
she gathered all at last.

1st voice   Magic fought magic; Christ's was the strongest.
Over the tribe-lands, the scatter of his settlements was a scatter of fertile seeds.

A Church took root and spread. The old worship was forbidden. The knives of blood-sacrifice rusted and grew blunt. Ancient words of power were silenced.

Yet here in the Celtic lands, the new faith dealt gently with the old. Sometimes it twined about the primitive stones, enriching them with the name of Christ and the mark of his cross.

2nd voice   It danced with the dancers, and let the candle-rays of its festivals merge with the torch-light of old processions.

It understood its people's bond with the Earth, and to her children it gave back the Mother, in her gentlest shape—as Mary the Mother of Christ, or as his foster-mother, St Brigid of Ireland, Sant Ffraid of Wales.

She it was who, story by story, miracle by miracle, was fashioned by the Celtic peoples into the saint of their desire.

She it was of whom one of her poets was to
    sing,
3rd voice   'Her name among created things
is Dove among birds,
vine among trees,
Sun among stars.
Her father is God,
her son, Christ,
her fosterer, the Holy Ghost.
It is she that helpeth everyone
that is in straits and danger:
it is she that abateth the pestilence:
it is she that quelleth the rage and storm of the
    sea.
She is the prophetess of Christ:
She is the Queen of the South:
she is the Mary of the Gael'.

PART II

1st voice   Sant Ffraid, to you we called,
seeing behind you the fiery shape
half-hidden in mist, and you
turning to embrace it.
Sometimes we scarcely knew
which Brigid we saw.
When we invoked you,
our words were shadowed by older words
of older prayers. Your emblems
were laden with ancient meanings.
Half-understanding,
we offered God our prayers through you,
letting you translate them
into his language.

2nd voice   On the few facts, the small foundations,
faith built a fabric of living fantasy,
pillars and pinnacles, a shrine for the saint.
All hopes had a home there, all prayers a place;
lavish was the love of Bride the beautiful.

3rd voice   Sant Ffraid, we made you
incantations at ancient wells,
begging you to heal us of mote in the eye,
measles and malice: to heal our beasts
of sickness in udder and hoof.

1st voice   Sun and water, all creatures of earth,

and all impulses of man the maker,
were brought into the compass of your care.

Eagerly we enriched your legend
with golden traditions; you wore them,
like torques and armlets, for our joy
and the glory of God.

2nd voice   We told of the oyster-catcher, who is your
        page,
plump and discreet in black and white,
stepping delicately behind you on the shore
on his long pink legs, or standing
one-legged to await your command.
Sometimes he stares down with gold-brown
        eyes,
and darts his long orange-red bill
down for his prey.
Sometimes he cries out, shrilly and sadly,
from the grey shingle, or flying over grey
        waves.
He wanders our world in otherness,
we cannot interpret his speech.
But he is your servant, Brigid,
encompassed by your understanding.
When death comes, not uncounted he lies
draggled on wet pebbles.
You have carried his cry to God.

3rd voice   We told of your fishes, the little brwyniaid—
how you filled the seas of Môn

with shoal after shoal, leaping to the nets
of starving fisherfolk who called on Sant Ffraid.
By thousands the fish came thronging, each one
small, long-bodied, large-scaled, strong-
   toothed,
with outthrust jaw, and a strange scent of
   rushes,
sacred to Brigid.
Nothing these beings knew of the miracle,
as the gasping of their gills weakened
and their twisting bodies were stilled.
The death of your creatures the brwyniaid
was not denied to them in their season,
nor life to your suppliants, whose hour was not
   come.

1st voice   Brigid, we sought strength
in your symbols of plenty,
weaving with reverence
the cross you had woven,
the cross of rush and the cross of corn,
visible prayer of humble hands.

We broke bread with our kin
and set your cross in the house-roof,
in beast-house and barn,
for blessing on labour,
on creatures, on home.
We trudged into winter, and through it,
toward your feast-day again,
and at last the return of the sun.

You had been with us;
all we could do had been done.

2nd voice   You were named poet and guardian of poets.
Yet great Patrick of Ireland, whose potent words
woke the love of God within you, saw devil's
work in the poets' power. He forbade them the
rites of magic and the utterance of judgments in
poetic language of ever-deepening darkness.
But much was left as the domain of poets, and
they were greatly honoured.
Theirs was the work of praise and satire, of
making genealogies, of laying down laws for
poetry, or composing lays that told of

3rd voice   'demolitions,
1st voice   cattle spoils,
2nd voice   courtships,
3rd voice   battles,
1st voice   killings,
2nd voice   combats,
3rd voice   elopements,
1st voice   grants,
2nd voice   encampments,
3rd voice   adventures,
1st voice   tragedies,
2nd voice   plundering'!

Since, in days before Christ came to the
            tribelands,
men had hailed Goddess Bride
as poet and muse, now they gave poetry

into your care, Sant Ffraid.
All its diverse themes you encompassed
and all its modes,
whether it gave delight
by a pattern of intricate metres,
or flowed pulsing like a spring
obedient to the heartbeat of the earth.

1st voice   And at your healing wells
you gently accepted the humble chant of your
     children,
whose unskilled verse grew garbled
to jigaboo and frimpanfree.
For you could hear
the silent flawless hymn
of their need and their faith.

2nd voice   It is fitting that you
should be saint of poets.
You are fire, as a poem is,
element of the phoenix.

Power sprang in you
like flame, unwilled.
The wooden altar-pillar
you touched in kneeling
grew green, took root, lived for ever,
sustained by your invisible
and unconsuming fire—
a useless miracle, a glory.

3rd voice   It is fitting that you
should be saint of poets.
You are mysterious, as a poem is.
We cannot say of you
she is exactly this or that,
or name with certainty your origin,
or set limits to your meaning.
You were a poem waiting to be written.
Found and revealed,
you make for us
resonances with things nameless,
deep, ancient and to come.

PART III

1st voice   Once fishing-boats at sea
would bow their sails to honour
Bride's shrines on the coast.
For the fishermen let down their nets
in the name of God; the tides
chimed the hour of prayer.
Work and worship mingled
like misty shore with misty sea.

2nd voice   And round the coast,
though now no longer on her day do folk
set shellfish at four corners of the house
and beg her help with the sea's harvest,
still her name lives in a scatter of sanctuaries,
and at the Stacks of St Bride in her great Bay

the snake-necked cormorant goes fishing,
and seals rise, sleeking off the streaming sea.

3rd voice Those who seek find legends
of lost chapels, obscure wells
and part-forgotten customs—in Môn,
the mothering island, or at Nevern
in the west, where her old chapel stood
at Henllys, and pilgrims bringing gifts
came hopefully dew-dabbling through the grass
of Pant Sant Ffraid.

1st voice Doggerel tells of a desecration:
'When St Bride's chapel a salt-house was made,
St Bride's lost the herring trade'.
Lost was the chapel too, from the shore of the
    Bay.
The sea rose over it, swallowed the salt
into its huge cleansing saltiness,
wrenched stones wetly apart,
then grudgingly sank back,
dragging ruin with it.
Tilted gravestones peered up
from blinding sand, and that was all.

2nd voice 'St Bride's, Llansantffraid'—
in her old valley-parishes
and on the hills, her name
strikes like a bell through silence
or lingers with a bell's insistence
behind the traffic of great roads.

3rd voice　　In her churchyard by the Usk
　　　　　　humbly he lay down, her Swan,
　　　　　　her poet of light, accepting darkness.
　　　　　　But that great Ring of Light
　　　　　　was flung about him, and he woke
　　　　　　within the radiance his time-shadowed heart
　　　　　　in dream had apprehended.

Voices in　　Sing Usk, sing Ogmore,
unison　　　Elai and Elan, Afon Cain,
　　　　　　Conwy, Ceiriog, Dyfrdwy,
　　　　　　valleys of her churches:
　　　　　　sing hills of Elfael,
　　　　　　sing Severn Mouth, where the long wall of
　　　　　　　　water
　　　　　　rears up between two Celtic shores:
　　　　　　sing now to greet your saint of rivers,
　　　　　　saint of light!

1st voice　　And they, the families gathered
　　　　　　at the farmhouse hearth
　　　　　　on the Eve of Sant Ffraid,
　　　　　　what did they wait for?
　　　　　　What was it that drew near
　　　　　　across the muddy yard
　　　　　　that stood on the step
　　　　　　and knocked the house-door?

2nd voice　　They saw a girl, one of themselves,
　　　　　　bearing green rushes.
　　　　　　What did they ask into the house,

when the rushes were strewn,
the candle lit, the bed prepared,
and the cry went up,
'Come, Bride! Come, Bride! thy bed is ready!'

3rd voice   Life and light,
green growth, blood's warmth
they welcomed in Bride's name
into the hungry house amid ice-hard fields,
and knew not how many centuries
reached out through them
to the returning sun,
or what presences stood on the step
in the shape of the shivering girl.

1st voice   Now it is we, Sant Ffraid,
we of a later age,
who by your ancient symbols,
by their perennial meaning,
invoke your aid in all things,
changed and unchanging.

2nd voice   Feed us, we are hungry!
Warm us, we are cold!
Enlighten us, we are foolish!
Mother us, we are lonely!
Fashion us, we are incomplete!

3rd voice   Saint of fire, fiery sun, fire-gold flower,
milkmaid saint of the sheltering cloak,
saint of the snake, hear us!

Hymn to Sant Ffraid

Voices in
unison

We call you, Brigid of the serpent!

1st voice

Brigid of the snakes, on your day
the serpent comes out
from the mound where he lay—
the great archaic snake
comes to wake
life in earth, life in womb,
and the year from his tomb.

2nd voice

Lady of the serpent,
smile on those who are quick and shining,
who glide swiftly to their aim,
whose words dart and flicker
like the tongue of a snake:
endow them with mercy.

3rd voice

Help all who are devious and suspicious,
whose thoughts are convoluted,
who hide their softness and tenderness
inside a scaly metallic skin:
endow them with trust.

1st voice

Help all who cannot move lovingly, directly,
towards those who love them,
yet cannot leave them alone,
but weave around them cold coils
of enchantment and illusion.
Free not the victim only,
but also the enchanter,
caught in his own cold and winding dance.

3rd voice   Save us from the venom
of the snake of temptation.
Set your serpent to kill him
for he is death.

2nd voice   Brigid of the serpent, pray for us,
who beg for life!

Voices in   We call you, Sant Ffraid,
unison   saint of the sheltering cloak!

1st voice   Christ's foster-mother,
who took the new born on your lap
and wrapped him in your cloak:
Christ's white milkmaid,
smooth-palmed, neat-fingered at the teats
of the lean cattle, let your hands over ours
draw down rich milk.

2nd voice   Shelter the beasts in stall;
keep them from bottomless bogs
on the black moor.
Save the heifer straining at calf,
bring milk for the new life.

3rd voice   Quiet Brigid of the kine, protect
all young nuzzling creatures,
and all who are slow, kindly and heavy,
submissive to goading and herding.

1st voice   Shelter the splendid, who walk loftily
like noble bulls in their pride of power;
save them from stumbling.

Hymn to Sant Ffraid

2nd voice   Pity those who shy nervously
from all who approach them.
Still their trembling, white-handed Ffraid.

3rd voice   Teach discretion to the brash,
who blunder like young bullocks,
mindlessly buffeting the sensitive.

1st voice   Milk-white Brigid, pity us all,
spread your cloak about us,
gentle us, cherish, protect!

Voices in   Hear us, saint of fire!
unison

2nd voice   Saint born at sunrise, flame golden one,
who took for your flower dandelion,
sunshine of roadsides and waste places—
shine for us.

3rd voice   Saint of learning,
send your uncompromising light
to aid all scholars,
bent over curly manuscripts
or seeking through innumerable books—
point them the truth.

1st voice   Saint of poetry,
be the fiery dissatisfaction
in the hearts of your poets,
that wakes life in their lines.
Fire of Brigid, burn dead words.

2nd voice   You on whose tomb fire lived so long,
            heal with flame the icebound craving
            of the unwanted, the impotent and barren—
            hear them, heal them.

3rd voice   Protectress of the peat-stack,
            meet us where we kneel on the hearth.
            Give kind warmth of fire
            to us and our kin,
            like the outstretched hands of a mother
            taking our hands,
            like her arms sheltering us.

1st voice   Be in the midst of the house,
            be the mothering fire
            in the midst of the house.

Voices in   We call you now to walk on the riverbank,
unison   to break the ice, to free the river.
            We greet you now
            from your churches and your wells,
            from the cold sea-coast and the colder hills,
            with the immemorial cry,
            'Ffraid is come! Ffraid is welcome!'

Poem-Sequences

Land

1 The Song

The farm grew its own wood
   of tall conifers. Gales thinned them;
some teetered, roots ripping upward,
but could only lurch on to thin,
close-packed neighbours, making with them
precarious arches.

From fields above to fields below,
down through the wood's dimness, plunge
long mounded lines, lost enclosures' boundaries.
Digging, dragging, heaving, firming:
sun-sweat, snow-shiver: man and hill,
and the years turning, turning
on to dark trees, and hidden mounds
delimiting sour garths.
                       But at the wood's lower edge
expansive sweet-chestnuts drop their splayed fruit;
above, where sidelan fields border on hill,
is a beech-glade, gold now, hazed
with a haunting of bluebells in late spring,
intenser here than anywhere—a marginal,
useless acreage, where now
once-disregarded beauty carries
the song of the place.

2 Ploughing Team

First acre for the ploughman,
if he can make a plough
from first nail to last.

Second acre for the keeper
of the irons, sharpener
of ploughshare and coulter.

Two acres for the owners
of the outermost oxen,
lest the yoke be broken.

An acre each for the owners
of the inner oxen, graded
in pride of years and strength.

The singing acre for the caller,
who brings the yoke,
who yokes the oxen with due care,
who calls them, who all the hours
of their labour chants to them
lest their hearts break.

The black acre for the man
whose ox drops in the yoke,
its heart breaking,
its breath fading over the furrows,
death calling it away.

3 Cenfaes

This is a still place.
 The breeze huffs and puffs tinily,
an irrelevance. Below the hill
the stream is hidden, its chatter muted.

It was hard to find the way here.
Since I came last, a generation
has been born and grown. New spurs of forest
confuse direction. In old fields
new leys have come and gone.
Slimy wood of an old gate lies in a ditch;
new wire, steel-thorned, stretches taut
from post to fresh-cut post.

The house is no more decayed
than thirty years ago.
It has borrowed an adventitious life
from vegetation—fir-tree pressing up
to the gable-end, tangle of grass and leaf
in open rooms. The land is grazed,
erratically; even the forest,
darkly, sourly flourishing, was planned
and brought to birth. Across the valley
a gleam of white is a rebuilt house,
grey sheen a new barn.

Those who have lived up here
must have known stillness like this,
a pause in the land's long story, when the mind

accepts loss and looking-forward,
holds them, as the year holds winter
and sweet air of the summer hill.

4 Sioned

Before I took her to wife
I judged the land by yield, its contours
as workable or not, and all it grew
food, shelter or nuisance.

Then she came, smiling, over my threshold.
Sioned, Sioned, said the wind,
that I had never listened to before
except for warning of storm.
From the tyddyn's grudging windows,
creaking door, now when I looked I saw.

Red-brown leaves, that had been nothing
but hint of winter, were warm with her hair's colour;
and in spring the useless bluebells,
that fed no stock, and sent my sled askew,
were for joy now, being her eyes
beneath my gaze.

He had two years, our son, until
his playtime ended, and he lay
fevered and wasting, drooling out

the sips of cawl or milk his mother held
to his white lips. Those weeks
before he died seemed longer
than all his tiny life till then.

She has a way now, on the warmest day
or by the hot winter hearth, of chafing
hand on hand, as though wringing them,
or as if some chill can never let her go.
Stiffly, in duty, she moves from task to task,
lies in our bed.
Sioned, Sioned, cries the wind over the hill,
where close among grasses bluebell leaves
wait for the spring.

5 Landscape with Figures

Behind the house loomed crags of a ravine.
A breeze, shifting, carried watery echoes.
Everything was pervaded by the valley's
extreme, uncompromising beauty. I thought
that there, whatever in the weave
might be harsh, twisted, disproportionate,
must stretch and blend into a balanced pattern.

One man I met there then is dead.
Invaded by a dark he could not speak of,
he cut his life away. The farmer stayed.

Skilled with the whittling-knife, in solitude
he wakes from wood the beasts asleep in it.
Weather and men he meets with taciturn
competence, keeping his counsel, never
risking unguarded boundaries.

Sometimes I see them waving me goodbye,
standing on the yard, their valley lit
superbly by fitful sun, and now see too
how down the ravine white mist would roll
like mercy to cover the suffering house,
and the land's beauty, that was not enough.

6 January Road

Fog and frost are forecast. Cold
has already deepened. Bare hill,
forested hill, rear into mist.
Up the farm road go Landrover,
grey digger with red arm bent back,
blue pick-up. Murky air deceives,
imposing strange perspectives;
from across the stream, climbing vehicles
are magnified to closeness, have startling
immediacy, their colour changing
this weather of despair.

The Landrover is gone
into encroaching white; foot by foot
digger vanishes, like a python's prey;
noisily, little pick-up follows.
Over the mountain the last curl of road
to a ruined house and its living pastures
will be made before cold clenches
too rigidly for prising.
                        Ragged-fringed,
mist drifts lower. From far within it comes,
faintly now, purposeful hum of motors,
long crunch of wheels, clunk of shifted stone,
undaunted music of the bright machines,
already journeying into spring.

7 Silage

Ensiled, the summer grass
rots in black plastic to nourishment
for winter stock. They too
may find that a diminishment,
preferring thrust and juice of growing leaf
on muzzle and tongue, or munchiness
of a rich summer's aftermath
to tease and prickle the mouth.
But hunger does not quibble. Soon,
in white fields or draughty stalls, slavering
they will mumble this rankness, relishing

the soggy harvest of a froward season,
summer less than it might have been,
yet yielding from wind-beaten rainy green,
to fire and flavour winter months,
savour and ferment of hot life.

8 Rights of Way

He guardedly agrees
that the day is fine.
He wonders where I come from,
but will not ask. He thinks
I have left gates open,
and will check. Finding them shut
will not modify his mistrust.

Few make their way up here
to cross his yard between
old house and older barns; one
is too many. He feels as pain
this violation of land, his land,
by ancient custom and prescriptive right.

Diffidently, in cherishing sun,
I cross to the far gate.
Crouched by an ailing tractor,
sidelong he watches.

We are straitly buckled
into antagonistic roles,
but I wave. Slowly
he raises a hand; turns away.

9 Aspects of Stone

Sandstone country—
    not many miles from home, yet the land
has its own vocabulary,
half-alien; not another language,
but an unfamiliar dialect.
The farmhouse down the track
could sit as happily
in a cranny of our moors,
but looks across a steeper valley
to sharper slopes, that hint
at the cliffs not far upstream.

In our valleys, hedges are coaxed
into as rich a growth
as shrivelling wind allows. Here,
field is parted from field
by stone, not wood and leaf,
a pattern of walls diversifying
the texture of grass.

Pure hill-bred
or plumped by a lowland gene,
sheep, driven by impulses of the blood
we construe as cunning or stubbornness,
adapt to their terrain.

The men who work them
are guarded at first meeting
on another's ground;
they live by the idiosyncrasies
of their own patch. Yet they
are of one cousinry, different
from all outside that wary,
humorous, enduring kindred,
but from each other, varying only
as shale from sandy rock,
aspects of stone.

10 The Hedge

Down the side of that sloping field
were old hawthorn trees, tall, wild,
all that was left of a hedge, no use any more
to divide or shelter, with those gaps
between trees, those branchy arches, waist-high,
shoulder-high, framing field or stream.

Now, back-end of the year, farmer and boy
have cut the hawthorn, chain-saw groaning for hours,
great swathes of brushwood fringing a corridor
in which a few branches, spared, are being bent
into a new pleached hedge; stakes driven in,
wire strained, to make a flanking fence.

It will be a good hedge, woven to trim
density, bare slim boughs budding
here and there, pale yellow-green, next spring;
the year after, trying a tentative
blossom again. Before too long
there should be shade and windbreak.

One day, far on, someone may stand
where I am now, across the river,
and say 'That's the old hedge, all run to ruin—
but look at the way those branches frame
parcels and plocks of beauty! Look now—
next winter is the cutting-time.'

(In old deeds, small units of land are sometimes called 'parcels' or
'plocks'.)

11 What Then?

And if one cottage
grew the best carrots
or one holding
had the best oats
or one hut
was hag-haunted,
what then?

Even their stones
are scattered,
even their bounds
arguable, their people
nameless.

     The young
listen to different stories.
What will they tell
when the nights draw in?

There is the life
and telling of the life.
There is completing
and forgetting,
and the offering
of forgotten things.

Pennant Melangell Poems

To the remote Pennant Valley in Montgomeryshire came in the seventh century the Irish Princess Melangell, in search of contemplative solitude. After saving a hunted hare from the hounds of Prince Brochwel, she became the patron saint of hares, and led a community of nuns living on land given by the Prince.

I Hare at Pennant

(Note: The ancient life-symbol of the Hare became debased over the centuries. One of its later manifestations, the Trickster, is in this poem identified with the hare saved by Saint Melangell from the hounds of Prince Brochwel.)

I Hare have been the clever one,
up to my tricks, always a winner,
fooling man and beast—but not now,
not you, pretty lady, holy one.
You untwist my deviousness.
I huddle at your feet
in your garments' folds,
and am simple hare, fool hare, hunted hare.
I have doubled and doubled,
am spent, blown, not a trick left

to baffle pursuers.
A leap of despair
has brought me to you.

Cudd fi, Melangell,
Monacella, hide me!

. . .

'Seize him!' I cried to my hounds
(the best, I had thought, in all
my princedom of Powys).
But each time I chivvied them on,
the fools came squealing and squelking back.
So I rode into tanglewood,
my huntsmen after me,
the wretched scruff-hounds skulking off;
and she was there in the glade,
still as an image, still
as her carved Christ on his cross.
I pictured her alone with me,
but this was no girl from the huts
to be gripped and thrown aside
for a paltry coin, no absent warrior's
hungry wife. Cool as moonlight
this maiden waited on wet grass,
looking up at me with no fear, no blame,
and by her small bare feet,
panting and peeping, crouched the hare.

I saw how it would be; she'd get her land
from me, the prayer-girl, to make
a sanctuary here—and Powys
would go short of hare-meat
and the dark strong broth! I
would make my peace with the cringing dogs,
hunt forests to the north for other prey,
yet leave a thought behind me here
for her to shelter.

Cudd fi, Melangell,
Monacella, hide me!

. . .

Once I was Great Hare
and the Moon's companion,
and Easter's acolyte bearing the light.
Victim, I ran charred through heath-fire,
lay bloodied in last corn.
I was warped to hold the soul of a witch:
dwindled to trickster and buffoon.
Men dodge my real, unchancy name,
calling me cat-shanks, cabbager,
dew-fellow, cat-of-the-furze,
maze-maker, leaper-to-hill.

False, broken is my boast of winning;
I crouch in dread of the fangs.
All I have been, am, she shelters.
'Not I', she says, 'it is my Lord'. But she

37

is what I know, soft-robed saint,
gentle one, who heard my piping cry,

Cudd fi, cudd fi, Melangell,
Monacella, hide me!

II Cwm Pennant

1 *Patron Saint*

Within the girdle of her care she keeps
the farms of her narrow valley. Far upstream
one house is new, foursquare, boldly red,
others insubstantial grey,
across fields, at the foot of hills.
A stranger on the road has to peer
to catch the dark of windows without glass.

Within the girdle of her care she keeps her church,
its ancient round of holy land
under hanging woods, in sight
of wilder heights beyond;
its intricate gnarl, dark spread of yews
over tip-tilt slabs of lettered stone.
At her May festival one bell sounds.
Her people have got up early, and press in
to pray, generation on generation
with never a jostle, while small warm rain
gentles their waiting homes.

2 Iorwerth Drwyndwn (Iorwerth the Broken-nosed)

They say that he, Iorwerth the blemished one,
had a refuge here, where Dafydd his brother
killed him for the lands of Arfon.

They say that if
by conquest and the death of brothers
Iorwerth had lorded it over all
their father's lands, he could not inherit
(lop-nosed from youth) the name of King.

They say that men
still held the old, merciless
dogma—marred King, weak realm;
would not have much lamented
this death in the secret valley, being used
to culling blemished beasts.

They say that all,
kneeling by taper-light at the shrine,
would own themselves blemished,
their inheritance bought back for them
by mercy; would then go out shriven, and meet
again the ancient inexorable dark.

3   *Legends of Giants*

In these mountains are legends of giants;
Balaam, Owty, Rhuddwen, Myfyr.
Some were nameless, like the jumping giant
of Moel Dinmoel, who left a well
where he landed. Not gods,
not angels, they were vulnerable
in their disproportion, not at home
amid hills meant to be looked up to,
paradigms of grandeur and mystery—
but to them, footstools, springboards, offering
nothing bigger than themselves. Lumpy,
passionate, destructive, the giants lumbered
through the landscape, here and there
casually altering it with dropped loads
of enormous rocks, springs bursting out
where great heels crushed the hill.

One huge guilt-ridden creature—
outlawed maybe, slayer of his kin?—
came crashing to Cwm Pennant by cockcrow,
seeking sanctuary at Melangell's church,
where the scale of power had a different measure,
where he could be small, comforted,
and die, perhaps, into the innocence
he had always been blundering towards.

4 *Saint Melangell and the Green Man*

High on the roodscreen, the Saint's legend
has pride of place. In pleated robe
she stands between huntsman and hare;
the dogs will never catch it.
But the crozier she holds came later.
She was a hermit first, for years,
sleeping on a rock in the wildwood;
all round her, matings and deaths
in the fecund, perilous night.

The screen is carved with branches of oak,
plumply-fashioned acorns, that mean life,
completeness. It would be easy to miss
in a corner above the pulpit
the Green Man, wild leafy face,
huge eyes desperate to comprehend
what will be.
             The King of the Oak must die.
Pilgrim, pray for lovers; virgin,
with your verities, cherish deciduous joy.

Singing to Wolves

(a Border sequence)

1 Llanthony

'Why should we stay here
          singing to wolves?' said Llanthony monks;
and left for soft living at the daughter-house,
finding themselves unloved by the Welsh,
and jaded with beautiful desolation—
just what the first anchorites had loved,
such wildness a treasure, not to be spoiled
by intrusive felling and tilling. All
they wanted was to contemplate heaven,
and the hills (almost as high), with herds of deer
ranging their tops.
                    The tidied ruins
are a favourite summer place. On this
burning day only children have spirit
to dash under arches, burst from shade to sun,
shifting points of colour, as intense
as flowers in baskets hung in front
of the crowded restaurant.
                    One tiny girl,
dark-haired, cool in a blue dress,

stays apart; alone she kneels on grass,
in the shade of the chapter-house wall,
carefully picking daisies. Perhaps she,
who knows? in her generation will be one
whose love is given to the remote, solitary,
trackless; to risk-encircled beauty;
deer on the marches of heaven; the sweet
unprofitable singing to wolves.

2 Capel y Ffîn

The stone gives nothing but a name,
   initials, dates of birth and death,
and then a verse about the sweetness,
depth, of laughing. He lies, or she,
near a line of yews, whose twisted trunks—
one pot-bellied, splay-footed, others
goat-hoofed and pitted—seem
compatible with deep, wild, joyously
contorting laughter.
                    Odd and true
this remembering; sad
the rattling laughter of survivors,
stones in the river's heat-struck bed,
rolling, falling about, denied the depths.

3 Cwmioie

So hot! Colours are soft in haze,
long tawny grass round the tombs,
brown shoulders of boys and girls
sunning by the crooked church.
Built on tip-tilted rock, it leans
every which way, buttressed,
stable after its fashion, with an air
of kindly eccentricity.

Inside, in the cool, a man
lies asleep on a pew, near
the tablet to seventeenth-century
Thomas Price, who 'takes his nap
in our common mother's lap',
his dust a compatible neighbour
for the bronzed and breathing sleeper.

'Better death than long languishing',
says Cadogan's motto. Amen to that,
on this day of heat and sleep,
amen! But after no long sickness
three small girls of one house came home
early from play. From their black memorial
one-year-old Mary cries 'I was but young',
and claims eternal rest, being too tired
too soon.

The sleeping man wakes up. Outside
the sunbathers have gone. A breeze mutes heat,
scampers over the graves, and starts
a susurration of grass, not unlike
whispers or stifled laughter.

4 Merthyr Clydawg

Clodock; it sounds rustic, and English.
Clydawg; the lost Welsh is back. He seems
an off-beat martyr, killed for love,
out hunting, by a jealous rival; yet,
a prince who led in battle and prayer,
his story has a spice of miracle. Oxen
(helped by a broken yoke) refused
to drag his body over the ford, insisted
that here should be his burial-place.

In the church, the gallery's music-table
might be straight from Hardy. But Latin
on a dug-up stone remembers
'that faithful woman the dear wife
of Guinnda', who centuries back
lived in this place of shifting boundaries,
strife, loss, perpetual haunting, garbled names,
Welshness in the soil's depth,
unacknowledged riches,
uncomprehended power.

5 Michaelchurch Escley: Christ of the Trades

The mural is faded. Least defined
is the figure of Christ. He is a blaze
of pale flesh. All round him
are harder shapes, of axe-blade,
knife-blade, hammer-head, spoke, tine,
griddle-bar, saw-tooth. The blades
are turned towards him. One slanting sword
is poised by his right shoulder; its point
hovers just short of his skin. Scissors, shears
overlap the line of his arm; is he cut?
One hand, the right, presses his breast; the other
is raised, palm out—warding off, or giving
a left-handed blessing? He seems
menaced by aggressive sharpness, closing in
with intent to wound, the things of everyday
banding to shear, scrape, gash, destroy
the extraordinary. In stillness
he bears the encroachment, stands
pale on the dim wall, his body a window
letting enter invulnerable light.

Riding the Flood

(a memory sequence)

1 First

The first child born in the new house
   pulled herself up by the sill,
started to see shrubs, railings, the long
faraway shapes that were hills.
She squatted by the fire, chuckling
at the day-old chicks that crowded cheeping
on their layer of puddled paper; inhaled
the mellow cardboard smell of the box,
and the half-sweet tang of enamel leg-rings inside,
and built a brand new nest of enjoyments.
Unknowing, she launched echoes
where a lack had been, a nothingness;
made for the house its first memories
of childhood; joined herself to the future.

2 Pattern

I realise now
  the wall was low; then
it was twice my height—
mossy, shaded, sun-freckled.
No gap gave a glimpse of lands beyond.
All I knew was liking
the difference between dank stone,
plushy moss, on my pudgy hands;
the dimness branches made;
and the wall dancing
when they swayed in a sunny breeze.

Sometimes I pore over this pattern
stamped on my mind, just above
the gulf where even earlier years
lie lost. Shadows of branches
dance over mossy stone
of the long-ago wall.
The dark mild happiness stays.

3 Links

Some have said that by the pillar
  where Becket was struck down,
they felt not pain but a derangement

of nerve-ends, a distant echo of blows,
enervation like blood-loss.
                              And I
in a windbitten valley have laid my hand
on stone of old walls, and felt a held life,
all the remembering there is
of what was made in that starved place,
a barely accessible material memory
woken with a touch.

4 Inward Eye

Not 'bliss', certainly;
      more a vagary of the inward eye,
but clear, seeming to mean—what?
I'm not dreaming, but briefly seeing
the lowest foot or two of a broad
greeny-brown tree-trunk, heavily ridged;
knobbly root-spread, and beyond,
rusty, collapsing, the corrugated roof
of a shed. It's all completely neutral—
no fear, no happiness to give a clue.
I can't remember it. Does it wait
ahead? I'm not some astral shadow
haunting it; I know the scrapy feel,
on my hand's flesh, of the bark.
So is that, after all, a memory?

Let it go to join the other fragments,
broken landscapes of chance and no-recall
that can't be re-assembled, anyway
not here, not yet. Whatever sent me this
out of nothing can have it back for now,
till its meaning comes with it. Let it go.

5 Shards

Calling
    from Scotland a song
from Devon a ship.

A white house on a cliff,
the breathy radio that seemed
that June to be always wheezing out
the same song.

South—July heat,
white corridor, doors folded back;
below, white lane angled sharply
down to a wall of sea
extreme in its blue.
Across the fierce colour
crept one white ship.

Far in time and miles
my grandson finds by ruined walls
shards, blue and white; and an idea
their jagged edges cannot cut
of a life, whole in another summer.

6 Investment

I must have given something to that day,
  that bit of seeing, living; or how,
after so many years, could so trivial
a recollection yield such riches?
It's like investing a small sum
and long afterwards enjoying
the surprise of profit.
                          I remember
the steep dip of road to harbour,
houses with whitened steps, but chiefly
the waterfront café, red plastic making
a hot day hotter. Mixed with our coffee
were motor-boat smells, oily, metallic, hot.
That was the rainiest of rainy towns,
yet instead of a grey memory I've kept
one fiery day. Perhaps what I gave it
was just the feeling that most things lay ahead,
and some (enough) would probably be good.

7 Child in Red

Christmas was just ahead,
a coruscation on dark.
We stood by your window.
Down there, across the wet street,
was a small shop's haze of light,
and a child in red, coat-skirt swirling,
laughing up at her mother,
dragging at her hand.

My mind slid down a groove
many had worn smooth—
'I shall remember this when I'm old'.
Nothing said how ambivalent
remembering is, or how there'd be
this compulsion to run away
into distractions, small speculations,
like wondering what happened to the child.

8 Gods

It was a city that had lost its gods
and long forgotten them. There had been
sudden music at midnight,
multitudes of invisible dancers
whirling through the streets,
out through the gates, away.

'Your luck is not in Egypt',
said the fortune-teller,
frowning at my cards. I thought
of Cavafy's lines, his useless hopes,
his proud farewells. For all of us
the gods may leave, the devalued city
devalue others.

        But now, look!
your gods are returning, Alexandria,
they are rising from the sea.
Down there lilliputian crowds
excitedly mill, as if dancing back,
as if remembering with joy.
Huge god-rulers, their stone dry
after centuries, are borne along
to a new enthronement—a thing of day,
a thing of luck, surely this time
not to be smashed or squandered,
not to be drowned again.

(Note: The reference to the Alexandrian poet Cavafy is to his poems
'The God Abandons Antony' and 'The City'. The huge statues
recently recovered from the waters of Alexandria harbour were
driven slowly through crowded streets.)

9 Riding the Flood

There are days when waves of unremembered life
    tumble in, one upon another, almost
irresistibly. You can feel the thuds
through the soles of your feet, through blood and bone,
all the channels and sluices of the body.
If the sea-wall gives, houses and a host
of little, loved, scruffy gardens will be drowned,
stay endlessly soggy and salt. Best
have your boat ready, furbish your skills
in navigation, submit to being lifted
higher than you could have imagined,
ride the flood, voyage to countries
you had given up hope of revisiting. Don't ask
whether that high tide of remembering
will ever carry you home.

Encounters with Angels

1 Angel with Orrery

Tall, with massive wings that have known
    abysses of the cosmos, he leans relaxed,
a rational angel benignly contemplating
a little orrery, and seeming
patient of its limitations,
approving, even, man's childish attempt
to model the unimaginable.

On measured rods and hoops of bronze
the planets march as wheels enable,
conjectured laws dictate. The angel knows
he is not to share with mankind
more than it can absorb. He has come
bringing a question, perhaps,
to plant rewardingly in one brain,
or a new idea this time and place can receive.

That done, he will be gone, through black depths
and towering flames, passing unharmed
back to the adored source. For now
he rests, stretching a kindly hand
to spin the children's orrery.

2 Angel of Death

He lay waiting his time. It was no surprise
when the angel was suddenly there
by the weary bed. But I had expected
a splendid solemn being to lead him away.
Were it not for her wings (and even they
were unspectacular) this girl
might not have been an angel at all.
'Are *you* the Angel of Death?' I ventured,
unbelieving. 'I am this man's time',
she said, 'yes, I am what you call death'.
'You are not as I thought', I admitted.
But then he opened his eyes
and looked at her, seeing, I think,
the ordinariness of it all; and went away
as quietly as his unfrightening guide.

3 Resurrection Angels

(The diarist Kilvert was told that people used to come to the Wild
Duck Pool on Easter morning 'to see the sun dance and play in the
water and the angels who were at the Resurrection playing back-
wards and forwards before the sun'.)

These were not troubling the waters
    to bring healing. They were serving
no purpose. After the watch at the tomb,
the giving of good news, they were at play.
To and fro went the wings, to and fro
over the water, playing before the sun.

Stolid-seeming villagers stared
enchanted, watching sun dance and play,
light-slivers splinter water's dark.
In dazzle they half-saw
great shining shapes swoop frolicking
to and fro, to and fro.

                    This much was shared,
expected; day and place had their
appropriateness, their certainties.
The people had no words to tell
the astonishment, the individual bounty—
for each his own dance in the veins,
brush of wings on the soul.

4 Atheist Angel with Message

'Are you bringing a word from God?'
I asked. 'God is an unnecessary concept',
he replied, sleeking an iridescent wing;
'I'm just bringing a message'.
'Where does it come from, then?'
'Does it have to come from anywhere?
It's only a message! Here,
I'll give it to you—you can spend your life
working it out'. I put it away
for later. 'Why do you bother?' I asked,
'as there's no God? Do you just like
travelling? I mean—all those messages
from no-one, for nothing?' 'It's my nature',
he said, preening. 'That's what an angel does'.
He soared into evening air
warm as indulgence, blew away
on a burst of breeze like laughter,
sunset lighting his dwindling wings
with undiscriminating glory.

5 Angel and Invisible Tree

Jesse sleeps. Extruding a dynasty
   has overcome him. A stump
is all that remains of the Tree.
No worm in the wood's heart
has eaten away his dream
of branchy maze, richness, sure design.
The angel at his head is awake
to see for him, so the Tree
goes on climbing, blossoming,
its boughs full of birds, people, creatures,
stories, fantastications, bunchy fruits,
extraordinary treasures. It seems to deny
nothing but death, but the angel
sees that too—the Tree cut, stripped,
planted on a black height;
and budding, sprouting again
exuberantly, looming aloft
in curly fronded complexity.
Jesse need not wake yet.
With amazement, the angel sees.

(Note: The wooden statue of Jesse in St Mary's, Abergavenny is
thought to have formed the base of an entire missing tree, a design for
the old reredos.)

6 Angel with Wolf and Saint

The angel sits by the well
   communing with a wolf and a saint.
It seems like a long
recognising of each other.

The well is half-hidden in a stone shrine.
Steps go down to dark water;
walls are slimy, colder
than their many hartstongues.
Below the hill, in trees, is a future house;
its grey walls waver with branches seen
through them. The church, too, above the well,
is as it will be; look hard
and you may see yourself, marvelling
at its ancientness and sanctity.

The angel is kin to the wolf in his wild
innocence, troubling to man. But the saint
is more than ordinary, being holy.
He is not afraid of these beings,
though each is alien. One knows
earth, cover, hunger, mating-stench
and the blood of blameless killing; the other
lives in the eternal surprise of heaven.

All three sit quiet within
the saint's prayer, a blessing
like well-water, like the cool of leaves
wavering through walls that do not exclude.

7 Faceless Angel

Stone sword at his side, dog at his feet,
he has a small angel each side
of the stone pillow, to prop his head.
This one sits huddled up to him,
wings folded, robe in changeless folds,
slim hand just touching his mailed shoulder,
her head thrown back to gaze
imploringly upward, if she had eyes.
But the faithful have scrabbled for centuries
at her pretty face, to steal
some powdery take-away holiness.
The sculptor's image of a higher being
enduring lowly service is stronger now
by accident, faith itself having humbled
the little angel by revering her.

8 Crazy Angel

Asymmetrically set, lurching
across a tombstone, is a strange version
of a celestial being. He looks drunk
or a little mad. Perhaps the carver
tried for divine frenzy; all he managed
was this ungainly angel, who blears
at one splayed hand, seeming to count

his pointy fingers as reassurance
for a distraught mind.

                    Lettering
has worn away, lichened stone
has flaked. Nothing remains to speak
judgment or love, forgiveness, praise;
there's not the coldest record cut to last.
Only this half-crazed angel
has flapped in from the edge of a world
and stayed, a voice for the silent,
opening the niminy o of his mouth
to utter a constricted cry.

9 Angel with Crwth

I said to the angel with the crwth
    'My music is not as I would wish.
Share yours with me, play songs
half mine, on the lesser strings
that can be flattened or sharpened,
and if it may be, on the great strings
never to be detuned, that are not of time'.

But the angel replied
'Though I can play
on the great eternal strings

and on the lesser strings
that sing the songs of time,
I cannot share the lonely imperfect music
you, and you only, can send
to cry along the light-years
and wind through infinite galaxies
to reach at last its resolution
in singular elected joy'.
He turned, and was gone. Tentatively,
I began to play.

(Note: The C, D and G strings of the crwth – fiddle – traditionally
represented eternity, and were not allowed to be sharpened or
flattened. The other strings were for temporal things, so detuning was
permissible.)

Ruth Bidgood: An Afterword
by A. M. Allchin

I

Ruth Bidgood's first volume of poetry, *The Given Time*, was published in 1972. It had already been some years since she had come back to live in Wales and settled in North Breconshire. In the years that have followed, she has built up a substantial body of work (nine volumes in all), as well as contributing a book in prose to the study of local history in mid Wales – *Parishes of the Buzzard*. More recently, particularly since the publication of her *New and Selected Poems* in 2004, Ruth Bidgood's work has begun to attract attention more widely and in a greater variety of journals than before. This is particularly the case with the penetrating and original discussion of her work made by the American poet and theologian Bonnie Thurston in an article published in the Jesuit periodical *The Way*. Here for the first time we begin to see Ruth Bidgood's work from an international perspective.

Two reviews that come from writers who have long shown their appreciation for Ruth Bidgood's poetry – Merryn Williams, writing in *New Light*, and Anne Cluysenaar in *Planet* – demand our attention. Interestingly, they coincide in their choice of one brief phrase to sum up something that is characteristic of much of this writer's work: 'how different is real/from ordinary.' For Merryn Williams, 'the ordinary equals the myriad small facts which assail us every day; the real is the significant and life-changing'. Anne Cluysenaar takes us a step further: 'Ultimately the near, the seen, becomes all the more precious, even visionary, because of the huge realities that remain beyond focus . . . The near and the far are held in tension through such an image – neither is ignored but each intensifies the significance of the other. We feel, indeed . . . how different is real from ordinary.'

Something of this same tension – between the real and the ordinary, the everyday and the exceptional – is to be found in reviews that come from two writers who are, I believe, discussing Ruth Bidgood's work in print for the first time. Kate Keogan, in a long and perceptive review in *Poetry Wales*, writes: 'She gives precise, vivid descriptions of scenes and her emotional response to them, but always this leads to something more, something essentially unstated. It is this which keeps drawing the reader back, this awareness of something that can be detected by one's peripheral vision, but cannot be looked at directly . . . Time and again the reader finds her looking to express

> Not exactly meaning. What comes
> is a willingness not to ask for that –
> a sort of gratitude, a sort of love.

A somewhat similar point is made in a review by Matthew Jarvis, of the English Department of the University in Aberystwyth, to be found in *The New Welsh Review*. After an interesting discussion of one of the earlier poems by Ruth

Bidgood – 'Llyn Safaddan', a poem based on a legendary incident in a historic place near Brecon – he goes on to comment on 'Llansteffan', a poem that also finds us coming to the end of our ordinary capacities of description: 'Indeed, the power of place in Bidgood's poetic imagination becomes apparent to the extent that the qualities of landscape can be formed into a prayer when humanity runs out of words.' The reviewer concludes: 'it is in its intertwined response to the detail of particular human lives and to the geographical spaces within which these lives have their material being that the particular value of this collection lies.'

We can see something more of this quality now that Ruth Bidgood's major poetic work, *Hymn to Sant Ffraid*, has found publication in this volume. This ode for three voices, commissioned by the BBC early in 1979, has never been published in its entirety. Its publication now brings a whole new dimension of Ruth Bidgood's work into view. This is not only a poem written to be spoken but is also a poem that involves a major statement of the meaning of 'Celtic Christianity' – that elusive entity which has evoked so much interest, and at times disagreement, in the last 20 or 30 years.

Rereading the poem now, I have been struck by how much the situation of this subject in Wales has changed in the last 25 years. Asked in the early 1980s by an American friend, the director of an institute for spiritual formation, for an introduction to people in Wales who were seriously interested in this topic, I found it difficult to send him more than two names. How different the situation is today! Apart from the Centre for the Study of Religion in Celtic Countries now established at the University at Lampeter, there has been, in the last quarter of a century, a remarkable growth of interest in this whole area. This development has revealed itself in many different ways, not least in the rediscovery of ancient holy places. The church at Pennant Melangell, for instance, with its fine reconstructed twelfth-century shrine, has come to new life as a place of pilgrimage and healing. What is true of Pennant inland is true also of the island of Enlli, at the end of the Llŷn Peninsula – one of the most frequented places of pilgrimage in pre-Reformation Wales. Indeed, the whole peninsula begins to be seen as part of a pilgrimage way. Something similar would be true of the church in North Pembrokeshire at Nevern, on the way to St David's, with its early standing cross and home to the Irish monk St Brynach in the sixth century. All these happen to be places about which Ruth Bidgood has written in memorable ways over the years.

It must not be thought, however, that Ruth Bidgood's poetic concern has been primarily with places of such ancient but now renewed fame. More often, her particular interest seems to centre on places almost unknown, scarcely remembered at all. She has described herself as one who desires to 'give a voice to the voiceless', those who are otherwise forgotten. 'Little of Distinction', in her first collection, is the title of a poem of particular delight, which describes a village that reveals so much more beauty than the guidebook suggested. This makes it all the more striking that, when invited by the BBC to contribute to a series of broadcast poems, Ruth Bidgood found herself proposing the theme of St Brigid of Kildare – a Celtic saint from Ireland whose fame certainly spread to Wales where churches dedicated to Sant Ffraid are to be found in many parts of the country. It was only as she came to terms with the complexity of the subject that she began to suspect the many strands of its total meaning. Who is this Brigid? How are we to place her? Is she a historical figure of flesh and blood? Is she a triple goddess? Is she even a representation of three goddesses?

The poet herself replies to our questions with a brief statement placed at the head of her poem: 'This is an ode to a concocted Celtic saint – concocted in that a real person of whom little is known took on some of the attributes of a previous fertility goddess cum muse, and became the centre of a cult which expressed a number of perennial human preoccupations.' All these different elements in the Brigid story, and others as well, find expression in the stanzas of Ruth Bidgood's celebratory poem. With great skill and a remarkable sense of the complexity of the story, Ruth Bidgood gradually weaves together the varied strands of myth and legend that have gathered round the name of this woman, who, it is said, led an actual flesh and blood life in sixth-century Kildare.

Before we come to look at the poem in itself, I want to turn to the work of a recognized authority on early Celtic Christianity, particularly in Ireland and Scotland, Dr Mary Low, referring both to her major study, *Celtic Christianity and Nature*, first published in 1996 by Edinburgh University Press, and to a more recent article contributed to a symposium on the nature of Celtic Christianity, *Celts and Christians: New Approaches to the Religious Traditions of Britain and Ireland* (Mark Atherton (ed.), 2002). I make this comparison because it seems to me that Mary Low's writing combines, in a remarkable way, academic accuracy with imaginative insight and understanding into much that relates to early Celtic Christianity and the natural world. My second reason for referring to her work is my sense that she seems constantly to be able to find a middle way through the often one-sided controversies that can plague this subject of the faith and spirituality of the Celtic world. My third reason is that her approach to the topic is in many ways closely akin to that which grows from the poetic intuition of Ruth Bidgood herself. What is particularly interesting is that Ruth Bidgood had, of course, not read Mary Low's book at the time she wrote the poem. Needless to say, neither had Mary Low read the poem published here. The fact that the studies of the historian and scholar on the one hand and the intuition of the poet on the other so often support one another seems to me highly significant and encouraging.

As already suggested, we are dealing here with a central figure in the early centuries of Celtic Christianity, a saint in Ireland whose fame spread throughout the Celtic world. Is there any real historical evidence lying behind the many and varied strands that go to make up the overflowing legend of this saint?

In approaching this question Mary Low writes:

Doubts are often raised about whether St Brigit ever existed. The Brigit who appears in the hagiographies could well be a Christianised goddess and nothing more, but it is difficult to be certain that there is not a mortal woman hidden somewhere in the depths of the Brigit myth. For practical purposes it was the Brigit of faith who mattered to her Christian followers. To them, she was a friend in high places, a power to reckon with, and a saint who was at least as interested in farms and domestic matters as she was effective in prayer and leadership. (*Celtic Christianity and Nature*, p. 159)

In her more recent article, Mary Low expands on this point:

> One of Brigit's character traits as a young woman is to be always giving things away; bacon to a dog, butter to the poor, her father's sword to a beggar. Sometimes the things she gives away are miraculously replaced or multiplied, as if God were both rewarding her and egging her on. (*Celts and Christians*)

However, these constantly repeated acts of generosity, so prominent in the earliest Life of the saint, are in the end only one strand in the story of Brigid. There are always more strands to be considered.

So, Mary Low can write:

> Brigit the saint inherits a great deal from Brigit the goddess as most scholars would agree. Brigit the goddess is not a single figure however, there seem to have been several different Brigits, many of whom have an association with fire. These Brigits, daughters of the Dagda, are described in *Cormac's Glossary* as the goddesses of poetry, leach-craft and smithcraft.

The work of the smith certainly involves fire; fire would also be involved in leachcraft, in the preparation of remedies and potions. 'Sunlight also has curative properties and can help to heal wounds, skin conditions and seasonal depression.' Beyond all this, gifts of fire and light are surely essential to the task of the poet.

In this context, some of the early Irish texts speak of poetry as 'a great knowledge which illumines/enkindles'. The author of the work known as *The Cauldron of Poesy* imagines poetry as a sort of inner light or fire that, so he says, each person has within them, but only 'in every second one does it shine forth'. The image here is of an inward illumination rather than an outward physical one; something deep in the human heart and mind that can reveal itself in speech and song and can be shared between those who can cultivate this gift and those not as able to do so.

In the end, through the many strands that go to make up the story of Brigid, we find ourselves coming back to the historical figure who lived in Kildare in the sixth century and astonished her contemporaries by the quality and quantity of her generosity. Certainly she takes on a great many roles, as her story grows: she becomes the 'foster-mother of Christ', assists his mother Mary in the inn at Bethlehem; she becomes the 'Mary of the Gael'. She is closely associated with fire – not only the fire of the imagination but also the fire that was part of the daily life of the church she founded in Kildare. One of the earliest Welsh testimonies to this aspect of Brigid's renown comes at the end of the twelfth century from Giraldus Cambrensis, who tells us, in a matter of fact way, about that fire as something he had seen and enquired about: 'It is not that it is strictly speaking inextinguishable, but that the nuns and holy women have so carefully and diligently kept and fed it with enough material, that through all the years, from the time of the virgin saint it has never been extinguished.' Something of the power of that flame comes to life in a new way as we follow the development of that story into the heart of Ruth Bidgood's poem.

It is fitting that you
should be saint of poets.
You are mysterious, as a poem is.
We cannot say of you
she is exactly this or that,
or name with certainty your origin,
or set limits to your meaning.
You were a poem waiting to be written.
Found and revealed,
you make for us
resonances with things nameless,
deep, ancient and to come.

II

There is much more to be said about both the person of Brigid
and the poem that celebrates her, but now we must turn to
the second element making up this new publication. This is a
group of 'sequences' – short collections of poems that, clearly
in the poet's mind, are linked together in a variety of ways
and need to be seen in relationship with one another in order
to have their full effect. Reading the five sequences to be
found in this book can be something of a revelation, even to
those who already know and admire Ruth Bidgood's work,
for, though many of the poems they contain have already
appeared in earlier collections and three of the sequences
themselves have been published in their entirety, it is perhaps
only when we see them together that we can fully appreciate
the impression they deserve to make.

Ruth Bidgood: An Afterword

This is the case particularly with the two longest groups of poems published here – the first called simply *Land* and the fourth called *Riding the Flood*, with the subtitle *a memory sequence*. Both are dealing with subjects central to Ruth Bidgood's writing as a whole: land and memory.

The longest of the sequences, *Land*, celebrates the life and work not so much of named and known places as the whole area of mid Wales Ruth Bidgood has made her home. In it we see something of the land itself and the daily work of the land: ways of work that, though constantly changing, have behind them very old traditions. We see this for instance in 'Ploughing Team' – a poem that takes us back into the remote past to medieval practices involved in making up the fullness of a plough team.

However, this sequence in no way hides from us the hardness of work on the land, nor its openness to grief and loss today. We see this in the poem 'Sioned' and still more in the case of 'Landscape with Figures'. Here the poet's impression that the very beauty of the placing of a farm would do something to mitigate the hardness and loneliness of its situation proves to have been mistaken. Of the two men who worked together there, one is no more.

> One I met there then is dead.
> Invaded by a dark he could not speak of,
> he cut his life away.

We discover that the land's beauty 'was not enough' in itself.

Not all the poems in this sequence are dark and threatening. 'Rights of Way' gives a wonderful picture of a wary farmer encountering a visitor he does not know – some kind

74

of tourist who, he feels sure, will certainly be up to no good. The humour and the detail to be found in the account of this momentary encounter of two worlds is characteristic of the poet's powers of observation and description at their best.

No less striking is the next poem in the sequence, 'Aspects of Stone', which reflects the way even small differences in stone, particularly building stone, can give a particular character, a particular flavour to a whole district. Yet these small differences are often held together within a general similarity of background and terrain. Thus, these 'aspects of stone' are mirrored in local differences of other kinds, particularly in the differences between the people who live and work among them.

> The men who work them
> are guarded at first meeting
> on another's ground;
> . . . Yet they
> are of one cousinry, different
> from all outside that wary,
> humorous, enduring kindred

The whole of this sequence – 11 poems in all – in the end creates a wonderfully truthful picture of the land and its inhabitants; a way of life certainly changing and threatened, yet still varied and alive and, somehow, unexpectedly, rooted and enduring.

To move from this first to the fourth of the sequences, *Riding the Flood*, is to move from one world to another. Here, the poet is telling us something about the inward world of memory as she knows it in herself. The fact that Ruth

Bidgood is deeply impressed by the way in which outward things – places, houses, ruined cottages – can act as containers for surprisingly ancient memories is here illuminated by poems that speak, for the most part, of the inner power of memory as it is known in her own life. We meet here with sharp, sometimes brilliant moments of recall from early childhood, cherished but challenging in their unexplained distinctness. We find, too, later and more extended memories that stick in the mind and can have their own reward in the present.

> I must have given something to that day,
> that bit of seeing, living; or how,
> after so many years, could so trivial
> a recollection yield such riches?
> It's like investing a small sum
> and long afterwards enjoying
> the surprise of profit.

In a sequence that deals much with small and private memories, it is at first surprising to come across a poem that takes us back to a much more public recollection – to the poet's years as a coder in the Navy during World War II, years spent partly in Alexandria.

> 'Your luck is not in Egypt',
> said the fortune-teller,
> frowning at my cards . . .

The city in those years of war, half a century ago, could often seem busy, full of frenetic activity, yet somehow forgetful of the riches of its past.

. . . I thought
of Cavafy's lines, his useless hopes,
his proud farewells. For all of us
the gods may leave, the devalued city
devalue others.

This memory of wartime dislocation is transformed by a more recent vision of Alexandria – the sight in a news film of a procession through the streets of the gigantic classical statues that had been recently rediscovered in the ancient port of that once great city.

Huge god-rulers, their stone dry
after centuries, are borne along
to a new enthronement . . .

The renewing power of memory, both private and public, whether in the dry colours of Cavafy's city taking us back into the heart of the Classical world or the green hills and valleys of the mid Welsh borders, with their own memories of a thousand years, is constantly surprising. That surprise is expressed at its strongest in the last of the poems of this sequence, *Riding the Flood*.

Best
have your boat ready, furbish your skills
in navigation, submit to being lifted
higher than you could have imagined . . .
ride the flood, voyage to countries
you had given up hopes of revisiting.

Of the remaining three sequences, two are devoted to par-
ticular historic places and, in that sense, are perhaps typical
of some of the underlying themes that run all the way
through Ruth Bidgood's poetic production. There is here a
sequence devoted to the church at Pennant Melangell – that
special church in its upland valley in the Berwyns, to which
we have already referred. It was only in 1992, when the
church was finally repaired and reordered for worship, that
it began again to become a regular place of pilgrimage. Two
poets were quick to respond to its story and, in the following
two years, poems by Glenda Beagan and Ruth Bidgood were
published illustrating the nature of the place and the power
of its story of Melangell and the Hare.

However, I do not think many at the time would have
anticipated that within the next decade a whole anthology
of poems relating to the place and its story would have
been published. The book – *The Hare that Hides Within*
(2004) – is the work of ten poets, four men and six women,
all of whom, from a great variety of viewpoints, have been
drawn to reflect on the story of the encounter of the hunts-
man and the hunt on one side and the solitary woman of
prayer on the other. As the Archbishop of Canterbury, in his
foreword to the collection, comments: 'These poems build
their own kind of shrine, like Pennant itself; a place to stand,
where you can resist whatever huntsman is in pursuit.'

When we come to Ruth Bidgood's sequence on angels, we
come to a subject that, though it has remained in some sense
on the edge of her attention, has, since her 1978 collection
The Print of Miracle, never altogether disappeared from
view. There in that third collection is a poem called 'Icono-
clast', in which a Puritan extremist recounts the havoc he has

caused in various East Anglian churches, breaking down images and blotting out pictures. Then, in his dreams at night, his sleep is broken. He finds in sleep:

> The great Angels he had left for dead
> still cried aloud God's message
> in the forbidden language of beauty.

In the present sequence – with the possible exception of the poem about the Resurrection Angels reported in Kilvert's diary, which seems to reflect a local communal experience – it is striking that each angel is different, each one strongly individual; the angel of death, so gentle, so unexpected, for instance, the atheist angel equally unexpected, who nonetheless has a message to bring as 'that's what an angel does'. More complicated is the poem 'Angel with Wolf and Saint'. Here we find that the angel has it in common with the wolf that he is in some way a unitary being, 'kin to the wolf in his wild innocence'. It is the saint who is in the middle who holds the three together as they

> sit quiet within
> the saint's prayer, a blessing
> like well-water . . .

This same calling to bring together different levels of things in unity, to work through what is imperfect, is clearly characteristic of the human musician, in the last poem, 'Angel with Crwth'. Here, it is the human player, the human poet, who has to work with 'the lonely imperfect music', in the end bringing it:

to reach at last its resolution
in singular elected joy.

I find it very striking that the poet has come so close in her
intuitive approach to the subject of angels to the common
conviction of the theologians of the Middle Ages, that angels
are subsistent forms, 'each differing from the other and form-
ing a species in himself' (*Oxford Dictionary of the Christian
Church*). They somehow accompany and assist us in a great
variety of unexpected ways, these poems clearly suggest.
Once again the writer's sensitivity and at times almost
humorous sense of proportion and disproportion makes of
these poems something strongly convincing and strangely
moving.

The end of this angel sequence brings us back to the point
of 'singular elected joy', thus also bringing us back to not
only the form but also the substance of the major poem that
gives its name and nature to the present volume, *Hymn to St
Ffraid*. This is not only a poem that has as its subject one of
the central figures of the early Celtic Christian world, but is a
poem that has as its substance the central matter of the whole
Celtic poetic tradition – praise: the praise of God above all,
expressed in and through the praise of his whole creation, all
the elements of the goodness of things. Here indeed there
are 'Symbols of Plenty'. Waldo Williams, the Quaker poet of
the mid twentieth century, says of his mother (in Rowan
Williams' translation):

She moulds afresh in praise the early morning unspoilt
    world.
(*ailgreu a'i fawl ddilwgr fyd*)

So, in the *Hymn to St Ffraid*, the poet has given us a whole, sustained symphonic hymn of praise, giving back to us an unspoilt world. We receive in these pages a particular gift, a gift hardly to be expected in our late and troubled time, and yet a gift truly given and truly made in and through the circumstances of the end of one millennium and the beginning of another.

So, we are enabled to call on the saint in this age, no less than in former ones:

Be in the midst of the house,
be the mothering fire
in the midst of the house.